DUBAI
FACTS

A Comprehensive Guide
with Fun Facts That You
Can Read While Exploring
Dubai on Vacation

Tommy Smith

This Workbook Belongs To

_____

_____

The True Fun Facts About Dubai for You to Read, Learn New Things and Understand Dubai Better

Table of Content

INTRODUCTION AND HISTORY OF DUBAI

Dubai's history spans millennia, once a trading hub and fishing village. Bedouin tribes, particularly the Bani Yas tribe, settled in the area in the 19th century. Dubai was part of the Trucial States, under British protection until gaining independence in 1971 as a part of the United Arab Emirates (UAE).

The Emirati Dirham (AED) serves as Dubai's currency, divided into fils. It's pegged to the US dollar, providing stability for the economy and trade.

Islam is the predominant religion in Dubai and the UAE, influencing daily life, culture, and traditions. The city embraces religious tolerance, allowing freedom of worship for various faiths.

7

Arabic is the official language, but English is widely spoken, especially in business and tourism sectors. Due to its diverse population, other languages like Hindi, Urdu, and Tagalog are also commonly heard.

Dubai's evolution from a desert outpost to a global city is remarkable. Its diverse culture, rooted in Islamic traditions, harmonizes with a modern, cosmopolitan outlook. The Emirati Dirham's stability supports Dubai's economy, while the city's welcoming atmosphere and multilingual environment attract visitors and businesses from around the world.

110 FACTS ABOUT DUBAI THAT VISITORS WILL ENJOY

How well do you know Dubai? Write it here.

(Before we start, write down all you know about Dubai so you can find out how well you know this beautiful city before and after reading this book).

_____

_____

_____

_____

_____

_____

_____

_____

_____

_____

_____

_____

1. Burj Khalifa: Standing at 828 meters, it's the tallest building globally, offering panoramic views.

2. Ski Dubai: An indoor ski resort within the Mall of the Emirates, where you can ski and snowboard indoors.

3. Palm Islands: Man-made islands visible from space, shaped like palm trees, hosting luxury resorts and residences.

4. Gold Souk: A bustling market where you can haggle for gold and jewelry.

5. Dubai Mall: The world's largest mall featuring an aquarium, ice rink, and over 1,200 shops.

6. Seven-Star Hotel: The Burj Al Arab, often called a seven-star hotel, is renowned for its opulence and luxury.

7. Desert Safaris: Visitors can experience thrilling dune bashing, camel rides, and traditional Bedouin-style camps.

8. Dubai Fountain: Adjacent to Burj Khalifa, it's the world's largest choreographed fountain.

9. Traditional Culture: Explore heritage sites like Al Fahidi Historical Neighborhood and Dubai Museum.

10. Cultural Diversity: Experience diverse cuisines, cultures, and traditions due to Dubai's multicultural population.

11. Jumeirah Beach: Offers pristine white sands and clear waters, perfect for relaxation and water activities.

12. Dubai Frame: A modern architectural marvel providing panoramic views of the city's past and present.

13. Global Cuisine Hub: The city boasts world-class restaurants offering diverse international cuisines.

14. Ferrari World: Not in Dubai but close by in Abu Dhabi, home to the fastest roller coaster globally.

15. Year-Round Sunshine: With over 300 days of sunshine annually, it's a paradise for sun-seekers.

16. Luxury Cars: Dubai's streets showcase a collection of high-end cars, including Lamborghinis and Bugattis.

17. Tax-Free Shopping: With no value-added tax (VAT), shopping in Dubai becomes even more enticing.

18. Dubai Opera: Known for its stunning architecture and a venue for world-class performances.

19. Palm Jumeirah Monorail: Offers fantastic views as it connects the Palm Jumeirah to the mainland.

20. Cultural Festivals: The city hosts various cultural festivals celebrating art, literature, and music from around the world.

Now Let's Test Your IQ

Without checking the book, write down 20 facts that you just read about Dubai.

1_____

2_____

3_____

4_____

5_____

6_____

7_____

8_____

9_____

10_____

11_____

12_____

13_____

14_____

15_____

16_____

17_____

18_____

19_____

20_____

How many times did you get correctly?

1st Try	2nd Try	3rd Try	4th Try	5th Try	6th Try	7th Try

Which is your most favorite of all these facts?

21. The World Islands: An artificial archipelago shaped like a world map visible from space, adding to Dubai's unique geography.

22. Luxury Hotels: Dubai houses some of the world's most luxurious hotels, including the Burj Al Arab and Atlantis, The Palm.

23. Camel Racing: Traditional camel racing remains a popular sport, showcasing the region's rich heritage.

24. Palm Islands: Among the world's largest man-made islands, the Palm Jumeirah, Palm Jebel Ali, and Deira Islands are architectural marvels.

25. Dubai Fountain: The world's largest choreographed fountain system, performing to various melodies daily near the Burj Khalifa.

26. Gold Souk: A market specializing in gold jewelry where visitors can explore and shop for intricate designs.

27. Dubai Marina: Offers stunning waterfront views, upscale dining, and vibrant nightlife.

28. Diverse Population: Dubai is home to a diverse population from various nationalities and cultures.

29. Dhow Cruises: Traditional wooden boats offering serene cruises along Dubai Creek or Marina.

30. Dubai Metro: The driverless, automated metro system is among the world's most modern and efficient transport networks.

31. Dubai Frame: This architectural landmark offers panoramic views of old and new Dubai.

32. Ski Dubai: A snow park within a mall, featuring skiing, snowboarding, and even penguins.

33. Dubai Creek: An iconic saltwater creek historically vital for trading, dividing the city into two districts, Bur Dubai and Deira.

34. Falconry: A traditional sport highly regarded in Dubai, often demonstrated at cultural events.

35. Multilingual Environment: While Arabic is the official language, English is widely spoken, reflecting Dubai's international character.

36. Jumeirah Beach: An iconic stretch of white sand offering stunning views of the Burj Al Arab.

37. Dubai Fountain: The world's largest choreographed fountain system, set on the Burj Khalifa Lake.

38. Dubai Miracle Garden: A vibrant floral oasis boasting elaborate landscapes and structures entirely made of flowers.

39. Traditional Souks: Places like the Gold Souk and Spice Souk offer a glimpse into Dubai's trading past.

40. Dubai Marina: A canal city with luxurious waterfront living, vibrant nightlife, and a stunning skyline.

41. Tallest Building: Dubai is home to the Burj Khalifa, the world's tallest building, standing at a staggering 828 meters.

42. Man-Made Islands: The city boasts stunning artificial islands, including the Palm

Jumeirah, shaped like a palm tree and visible from space.

43. No Income Tax: Dubai doesn't impose income tax on its residents, contributing to its attractiveness as a financial hub.

44. Luxury Police Fleet: Its police force includes luxury cars like Lamborghinis and Ferraris, reflecting the city's opulence.

45. Indoor Ski Resort: Despite the desert climate, Dubai houses Ski Dubai, an indoor ski resort with real snow.

46. Multi-Cultural Hub: It's a melting pot of cultures; over 85% of its residents are expatriates from various countries.

47. Year-Round Sunshine: Dubai enjoys sunshine nearly every day of the year, making it a perfect destination for sun seekers.

48. World Records Galore: Beyond the tallest building, it's also home to the largest shopping mall and biggest choreographed fountain show.

49. Traditional Souks: Amidst modernity, old-style markets or 'souks' still thrive, selling spices, gold, and textiles.

50. Religious Diversity: While Islam is the primary religion, Dubai is known for its tolerance; visitors can find churches, temples, and mosques coexisting.

Score Yourself

Now it's time to score yourself. Out of the first 50 fun fact, how many did you already know?

Write 15 more facts that you've not yet read in this book but you know or just remembered about Dubai.

1._____

2._____

3._____

4._____

5._____

6._____

7._____

8._____

9._____

10._____

11._____

12._____

13._____

14._____

15._____

51. Robotic Camel Racing: Dubai once featured camel racing, traditionally popular in the region. Nowadays, robot jockeys have replaced human riders in these races.

52. World's Largest Gold Market: Dubai Gold Souk is a vibrant market where thousands of shops sell gold, making it one of the largest gold markets globally.

53. 24/7 Economy: Shops and businesses in Dubai often remain open round-the-clock, catering to the city's vibrant nightlife and diverse working hours.

54. Home of World-Class Hotels: Dubai hosts some of the most luxurious hotels globally, including the iconic Burj Al Arab, known for its opulence and unique design.

55. Artificial Rain: During scorching summer months, Dubai has been known to create artificial rain using technology to reduce extreme heat.

56. Falconry Tradition: Falconry is a significant tradition in Dubai. Falcons are highly regarded, and there's even a hospital dedicated to these majestic birds.

57. Underwater Tennis: Plans were once proposed for an underwater tennis court off the coast of Dubai, though it has yet to be realized.

58. Zero Crime Tolerance: Dubai is known for its strict laws and has one of the lowest crime rates globally, making it a remarkably safe city.

59. Cosmopolitan Dining: Dubai offers an incredibly diverse culinary scene, featuring cuisines from almost every corner of the world.

60. Tax-Free Shopping: With its tax-free policy, Dubai is a haven for shopping enthusiasts, boasting numerous malls and designer boutiques.

61. Ski Dubai: Despite the desert climate, Dubai houses Ski Dubai, an indoor ski resort located inside the Mall of the Emirates, offering snowy slopes and winter activities.

62. Record-Breaking Skyscrapers: Dubai's skyline is dominated by remarkable skyscrapers, including the Burj Khalifa, the tallest building globally, and numerous others that showcase architectural marvels.

63. Weekend Days: The weekend in Dubai falls on Friday and Saturday, with Sunday being the start of the workweek.

64. Art and Culture Hub: The city hosts various cultural events, including the Dubai Opera, where performances, concerts, and theater productions take place.

65. Taxi Fleet of Luxurious Cars: Dubai's taxis include a fleet of high-end cars like Mercedes-Benz and Lexus, providing a luxurious travel experience.

66. Palm Jumeirah: One of the world's largest artificial islands, shaped like a palm tree, it hosts lavish hotels, residential properties, and entertainment venues.

67. Camel Polo: An unusual sport, camel polo, is played in Dubai, blending the traditional camel riding with the essence of polo.

68. Public Transport: Dubai has an efficient and modern public transport system, including the Dubai Metro, making commuting across the city convenient.

69. Artificial Islands: In addition to Palm Jumeirah, Dubai is known for The World, an archipelago of artificial islands shaped like a world map.

70. Dubai Creek: This historical area served as a hub for trading and fishing and retains its traditional charm with its bustling markets and dhows (traditional boats) transporting goods.

Score Yourself Again

Without checking the book, write down 5 facts that you've just read about Dubai.

1_____

2_____

3_____

4_____

5_____

How many times did you get correctly?

1st Try	2nd Try	3rd Try	4th Try	5th Try	6th Try	7th Try

Which is your most favorite of all these facts?

┌─────────────────────────────────────┐
│   │
└─────────────────────────────────────┘

71. Falconry: Dubai has a deep-rooted tradition of falconry, and the city even has a hospital dedicated to falcons, providing specialized care for these majestic birds.

72. The Dubai Fountain: Located at the base of Burj Khalifa, this captivating fountain show is illuminated with vibrant lights and performs synchronized dances to music, attracting crowds every evening.

73. Luxury Shopping: Dubai is a paradise for shoppers, boasting extravagant malls like The Dubai Mall and Mall of the Emirates, offering a vast array of high-end brands and luxurious shopping experiences.

74. Food Diversity: From local Emirati cuisine to international flavors, Dubai's culinary scene is a fusion of diverse cultures, offering an array of delectable dishes.

75. Global Village: A cultural extravaganza featuring pavilions representing different countries, showcasing their cultures, cuisines, and crafts in one vibrant location.

76. Gold Souk: A bustling market in Dubai's old quarter, Deira, where you can find an abundance of gold jewelry and experience the lively atmosphere of a traditional souk.

77. Year-Round Sunshine: Dubai enjoys sunny weather throughout the year, making it an ideal destination for those seeking a warm climate.

78. Safety: Dubai is known for being one of the safest cities globally, ensuring a secure and comfortable environment for residents and visitors.

79. Artificial Rain: To combat the extreme heat, Dubai employs technology to generate artificial rain, contributing to temperature regulation.

80. Diverse Expat Community: Dubai is home to a vibrant expatriate population from around the world, contributing to its multicultural ambiance.

Another IQ test

Without checking the book, write down 15 facts that you just read about Dubai.

1_____

2_____

3_____

4_____

5_____

6_____

7_____

8_____

9_____

10_____

11_____

12_____

13_____

14_____

15_____

How many times did you get correctly?

1st Try	2nd Try	3rd Try	4th Try	5th Try	6th Try	7th Try

Which is your most favorite of all these facts?

81. The name "Dubai" has different origins: There are various theories about the etymology of the name.

Some people say that it comes from the name "money". They refer to the fact that those living here were very wealthy due to economic conditions.

82. Burj-al-Arab is the only seven-star hotel in the world: This is the tallest hotel in the world: Burj Al Arab. It has 321 meters and is situated on an artificial island. The island is linked to the other parts of the city by a 340 meters long road. It is known for its sky bars.

The Dubai Skyview bar broke the Guinness World Record for the most expensive cocktail. The price of the cocktail is approximately 7440 US dollars.

The cocktail is served in a Swarovski Crystalline cocktail glass. As a result, you can take the glass with you as a souvenir from this amazing destination.

83. Palm Islands are artificial: They are composed of three islands: Palm Jumeirah, Jebel Ali, and Deira. They have one thing in common. The Jumeirah island is already constructed. The Jebel Ali island is under construction. The Deira island is a new project which has not started yet.

84. The majority of the population are expatriates: Dubai has a good immigration policy.

They welcomed thousands of foreign workers in order to boost the economy. 85% of the population of this emirate are foreigners.

Everyone here is hard-working and live in a safe environment.

85. 70% of the residents are male: Gender equality is a problem in the Middle East. 70% of people living in Dubai consists of male. The majority are expatriates. They come here to work. However, the government runs projects to support motivated and educated women.

86. The green is the color of Dubai police forces: The luxe is everywhere in this great destination. Don't be surprised to see the brand new police cars. The cars and officers' uniform are in green. It is the dominant color of these forces. There are eleven stations in the city. Female officers wear a headscarf.

87. Dubai has veto power in the UAE: The United Arab Emirates were created in the 1970s.

The seven emirates, including Abu Dhabi and Dubai, formed the UAE. These two emirates made a condition to join the coalition. They are the only two emirates to have veto power over political and economic issues in the country.

88. Dubai is home to the second-largest shopping mall in the world:

The UAE is a famous shopping destination. There are more than sixty malls. Twelve other malls are under construction. The second-biggest mall is Dubai Mall. It is situated in the downtown of the city. It's one of the top places to discover in the UAE.

89. Burj Khalifa has 57 elevators: It's the tallest building in the world. Burj Khalifa has 828 meters of height and is situated in the Downtown. There are two observation decks here.

The highest one is situated on the 148th floor. There is a breathtaking view of the city and the skyline.

90. Ramadan is the most important period in the year: You should respect the local etiquette and culture. Firstly, it's important to adopt a respectful dress code. It's the best period to immerse in amazing cultural traditions and customs. You can directly participate in many charity events during Ramadan.

91. Dubai has the longest automated metro system: The metro system is completely automated without any drivers.

There are three classes in the metro: first or VIP class, women class, and ordinary class. The metro system is completely adapted to the high temperatures.

92. Dubai has unusual vending machines: The residents really love gold. There are ATM's that distribute gold bars. If you would like to buy eastern jewelry, you should absolutely visit the gold souk (market). It's a must-do place for precious stones and jewelry lovers.

93. Dubai has a tax-free system: One of the interesting facts about the city is that there is no income tax. But, in some circumstances, you will face a tax. The advantageous tax policy is one of the reasons why people travel to this destination for job opportunities.

94. Dubai fountains can perform: The dancing fountain is one of the biggest fountains in the world. It is located in Dubai on an artificial lake. Every evening you can admire the performing fountains.

The best places to observe the musical show are Burj Khalifa, Waterfront Promenade and Souk Al Bahar.

95. The desert in Dubai is the hottest in the world: The temperatures vary drastically between daytime and the night. The highest temperature ever registered reaches 49°. It's almost impossible to visit it in the summertime, especially in the afternoon. You can do things like camel racing, dune bashing, and sandboarding.

96. The World islands are under construction:

Dubai is breaking the stereotypes. The World islands is a new mega project off the coast of the city. It consists of 300 private artificial islands. It is in the form of the six continents. Currently, the project is under construction.

97. There is no zip code system in the city: One of the most interesting things in Dubai is that there is no zip code system.

A city that builds artificial islands and the tallest skyscrapers, didn't implement a simple zip code system. As a result, online shopping is a real brain teaser for post officers.

98. The end of the oil resources is near: Dubai has one of the largest amounts of oil resources in the Middle East.

According to some specialists, this resource will definitely run out in 2019 in the country.

However, it continues to be a major source of revenues and development in the UAE.

99. Dubai International airport has highly-developed facilities for passengers: It has an indoor garden called "Zen gardens".

Additionally, the airport has an entire terminal dedicated to A380, the world's biggest passenger airplane. There are sleeping cabins, called "Snooze cubes". You can pass your overnight in these comfortable rooms with free wifi connexion.

100. There is a minimal risk of natural disasters in Dubai: The overall area is safe from earthquakes and tsunamis. The explanation of this phenomenon is that the Persian Gulf waters are not that deep. And, even if the artificial islands are built up of sand, they don't represent any major safety risk.

Assimilation and Retention Level Test Instruction:

Now you've read and memorized 100 facts about Dubai.

Let's test your assimilation and retention level.

Without checking the book, in the next 10 minutes, write down 30 facts that you just read about Dubai.

Set Your Timer

1_____

2_____

3_____

4_____

5_____

6_____

7_____

8_____

9_____

10_____

11_____

12_____

13_____

14_____

15_____

16_____

17_____

18_____

19_____

20_____

21_____

22_____

23_____

24_____

25_____

26_____

27_____

28_____

29_____

30_____

How many minutes did it take you to complete this test?

```
[                                    ]
```

How many times did you get correctly?

1st Try	2nd Try	3rd Try	4th Try	5th Try	6th Try	7th Try

Which of these facts are most relatable?

43

101. Dubai is tolerant towards western cultures: The United Arab Emirates is a Muslim country. However, they are very open to foreign culture and traditions. The population of Dubai lives in perfect harmony. Therefore, tourists from western countries can travel across it in safety.

102. Dubai became a megapolis in 30 years: Before tourism and oil, it was an ordinary pearl diving village. The village didn't have even elementary living conditions. After the discovery of natural resources, the rulers decided to invest in infrastructure and tourism development.

103. Abu Dhabi helped to build the world's highest building: This has been a challenging project. Sheikh Khalifa bin Zayed Dubai who is the ruler of Abu Dhabi helped to finish the construction.

44

At first, the building was named "Burj Dubai". One day prior to the inauguration the rulers decided to rename it "Burj Khalifa".

104. The world's second largest indoor snow park: Dubai is the capital of contrasts. Skiing in an indoor snow park, then chilling in the desert is completely possible in this destination. This indoor ski complex provides snowboarding and ski lessons for friends and families.

105. 20 Years Ago, Dubai Was A Desert: Humans have lived in the United Arab Emirates (UAE) for 125,000 years. Yet it was not until the 18th century that the town we know today as Dubai was founded.

At first, the town was a small fishing village, with a population of just a few hundred people.

It was small and cramped, with most of the modern-day city being a desert.

Farmers wouldn't even use the land for growing plants or maintaining livestock because it was inhabitable.

In 1971, the United Arab Emirates was founded. The UAE became a wealthy nation virtually overnight due to its immense supplies of oil.

Oil was found off the coast of Dubai, so businessmen began streaming into the city to start businesses.

Though the Gulf War caused many business people to leave, they returned once oil prices rose. Starting in the 2000s, they invested in the development of Dubai, which continues to this day.

106. Foreigners Love Dubai: Dubai's population is just shy of three million people. Despite Dubai's importance to the UAE, only 15% of the population consists of native UAE residents.

Dubai has a massive population of Indian, Pakistani, and Bangladeshi residents. Many of these residents are businesspeople who moved to Dubai to pursue various opportunities.

You can find Indian and Pakistani communities and businesses spread throughout the city, especially in high-income areas.

The largest population of Western expatriates consists of British people. But you can find Americans as well as many people from Africa, particularly Somalia.

107. Weekends Are Not on Saturdays and Sundays: For years, the weekends in Dubai consisted of Fridays and Saturdays. In January 2022, Dubai changed its official weekends to align better with international financial markets.

However, their weekends and hours off are still a little different. Dubai businesspeople work between 7:30 a.m. and 3:30 p.m. from Monday through Thursday. They work until noon on Friday, and their weekends run until Monday morning.

108. Stay In Luxury: Dubai is perhaps the greatest city in the world for luxury hotels. Even if you are traveling on a budget, you can stay at a location with great amenities and personal services.

The Burj Al Arab has thousands of five-star reviews on TripAdvisor, yet you can stay at the hotel for as low as $200 a night.

You can use free high-speed internet, enjoy massages and manicures at the hotel's spa, and eat breakfast at a buffet. We stayed at JW Marriott Dubai and The Habtoor Grand Dubai they were both magnificent and quite affordable.

109. The Miracle Garden Is The World's Largest Flower Garden: The Dubai Miracle Garden contains more than 50 million flowers spread across 780,000 square feet of space. It is the world's biggest natural flower garden, and you find virtually every species of flower inside the garden.

The garden also contains the world's biggest floral installation, a life-size version of the

Emirates A380 made entirely of flowers. When you need to take a rest, you can sit down in the sitting area under a canopy of flowers and look at fountains.

110. You Can Find Wildlife In Dubai: Despite Dubai's rapid development, you can find many different animals in and around the city. As you might imagine, you can see camels and even go racing on them.

But you can also see falcons, wolves, leopards, and Arabian oryxes in their natural habitats.

You can travel outside the city to conservation centers, including the Ras Al Khor Wildlife Sanctuary. If you prefer to stay inside the city boundaries, you can go to The Green Planet, which contains an entire tropical rainforest inside a bio-dome.

70+ FREQUENTLY ASKED QUESTIONS FOR YOU TO ANSWER ABOUT DUBAI

What are people from Dubai called?

_____

_____

What can you do in Dubai?

_____

_____

_____

_____

_____

_____

What is Dubai famous for?

_____

_____

What language do they speak in Dubai?

_____

_____

What was the original name of Dubai?

_____

_____

Why do people love Dubai?

_____

_____

_____

_____

_____

_____

_____

Is Dubai a city or a country?

_____

_____

What are the historical origins of Dubai?

_____

_____

_____

_____

_____

_____

_____

What is the difference between Dubai and the United Arab Emirates?

_____

_____

_____

_____

_____

_____

Where is Dubai and in which country is it located?

_____

_____

_____

_____

What can you buy for AED 1 in Dubai?

_____

_____

_____

_____

_____

_____

Is Dubai cheap or expensive? Why?

_____

_____

_____

_____

Is gold cheaper in Dubai than elsewhere in the world?

_____

_____

_____

_____

What is the cost of living in Dubai?

_____

_____

_____

_____

_____

What salary do I need to live well in Dubai?

_____

_____

_____

_____

Are public displays of affection allowed in Dubai?

_____

_____

_____

_____

_____

_____

Can I drink alcohol in Dubai?

_____

_____

Can I wear shorts in Dubai?

_____

_____

_____

_____

_____

_____

Do women in Dubai have to wear a headscarf?

_____

_____

Can I swim in the sea in Dubai?

_____

_____

Can I tan in Dubai?

_____

_____

Can I live in Dubai?

_____

_____

_____

Do people pay tax in Dubai?

_____

_____

Is Dubai dog-friendly?

_____

_____

What can women wear in Dubai?

_____

_____

_____

What is the sea like in Dubai?

_____

_____

_____

Where are the public beaches in Dubai?

_____

_____

_____

_____

Are women in Dubai restricted in any way?

_____

_____

_____

_____

Is there anything prohibited in Dubai?

_____

_____

_____

_____

_____

_____

What are the rules during Ramadan?

_____

_____

_____

_____

Are restaurants closed in Dubai during Ramadan?

_____

_____

Can I visit Dubai during Ramadan?

_____

_____

_____

Do people give gifts during Ramadan?

_____

_____

How is Ramadan observed in Dubai?

_____

_____

_____

_____

Is Ramadan a good time to visit Dubai?

_____

_____

What should you wear during Ramadan?

_____

_____

_____

Do hotels operate normally during Ramadan?

_____

_____

_____

What are the rules for eating, drinking and smoking during Ramadan fasting hours?

_____

_____

_____

_____

Can you go to the beach and dine at restaurants during Ramadan?

_____

_____

What do I need to bring when visiting Dubai?

_____

_____

_____

_____

_____

_____

_____

Can I pay with euros in Dubai?

_____

_____

_____

_____

How much do I need to spend for a honeymoon in Dubai?

_____

_____

_____

_____

How much does a taxi cost in Dubai?

_____

_____

Is Dubai expensive as a holiday destination?

_____

_____

What is the cheapest month to visit Dubai?

_____

_____

_____

_____

What should my budget be for a week's holiday in Dubai?

_____

_____

_____

_____

Where can I take the metro in Dubai?

_____

_____

_____

What is the official language in Dubai?

_____

_____

How do you say "hello" in Dubai?

_____

_____

What languages are spoken in Dubai?

_____

_____

_____

_____

_____

_____

_____

Does Dubai get cold at night?

_____

_____

_____

_____

Does Dubai have four seasons?

_____

_____

_____

Does it snow in Dubai?

_____

_____

What is a good climate for a visit to Dubai?

_____

_____

What is the coldest month in Dubai?

_____

_____

What type of climate does Dubai have?

_____

_____

When is it cold in Dubai?

_____

_____

_____

How safe is Dubai for women?

_____

_____

_____

_____

Is anything prohibited in Dubai?

_____

_____

_____

Is Dubai safe?

_____

_____

Is it safe to walk around at night in Dubai?

_____

_____

_____

What items are not allowed in Dubai Airports?

_____

_____

_____

_____

_____

_____

I cannot remember my login details. What should I do?

_____

_____

_____

_____

_____

_____

_____

_____

Thanks for reading. I hope you've learnt something new about Dubai today...

Made in the USA
Monee, IL
04 March 2025

13456674R00039